Original title:
Silent Snowlight

Copyright © 2024 Swan Charm
All rights reserved.

Author: Sebastian Sarapuu
ISBN HARDBACK: 978-9916-79-435-7
ISBN PAPERBACK: 978-9916-79-436-4
ISBN EBOOK: 978-9916-79-437-1

A Canvas of Soft White

In winter's hush, the world lies still,
A blanket soft, a pure white thrill.
Footprints linger, a secret shared,
Nature's beauty, with love declared.

Icicles glisten under the sun,
Each glint, a story just begun.
A canvas vast, with dreams in tow,
A winter's art, forever aglow.

Treading on Whispered Dreams

In twilight's glow, we softly tread,
On whispered dreams, where hopes are fed.
Stars twinkle faint in the dusky sky,
We find our way, as time drifts by.

Through shadowed paths, we roam and weave,
Each step a tale that we believe.
In gentle breezes, our secrets dance,
Wrapped in the night, we take our chance.

Winter's Gentle Murmur

Listen close to winter's breath,
A gentle murmur, life and death.
Frosty whispers touch the trees,
Nature's song sways with the breeze.

Along the stream, a silence reigns,
With crystal clear, the stillness gains.
Nature's lullaby, sweet and low,
In winter's heart, the world will glow.

Elysian Fields of Frost

In fields of white, where time stands still,
Frosty patterns, a painter's thrill.
Every crystal, a dream unfurled,
A tranquil place, a hidden world.

Beneath the sky, so vast and bright,
We wander through this pure delight.
In Elysian fields, we chase the sun,
Forever lost, yet never done.

Frosted Dreams in Moonlight

In stillness wrapped, the night unfolds,
A tapestry of silver and gold.
Whispers of dreams on frosted air,
Where shadows dance, and none compare.

Beneath the gaze of a glowing moon,
The world holds breath, a sweet cocoon.
Soft glimmers touch the weary ground,
In this soft cradle, peace is found.

Stars sprinkle light on nature's sleep,
In frosted dreams, the heart will leap.
Wrapped in silence, fears take flight,
As hope ignites the velvet night.

The Hushed Embrace of Snowflakes

Falling gently, a delicate dance,
Each snowflake drapes us in a trance.
Soft whispers weave through the night air,
A quiet promise, life laid bare.

Circling patterns, a winter's sigh,
In this hush, the world draws nigh.
Blanketed in white, we find our peace,
In every flake, a sweet release.

Like secrets told in softest grace,
Snowflakes flutter, each finds its place.
In their embrace, warmth we seek,
Through chilly air, we softly speak.

Glimmering Veils of Stillness

A stillness drapes across the land,
Like velvet whispers, tender and grand.
Glimmering veils, a soft embrace,
In frozen moments, time finds space.

Echoes caught in a crystal glow,
As shadows linger, soft and slow.
In silence held, our spirits rise,
Beneath the vast, expansive skies.

Each breath we take, a crystal fine,
Where dreams align in soft design.
Glimmering veils, the heart's delight,
Hold us gently through the night.

Shimmering Twilight on Blankets White

Twilight beckons, a soft reprieve,
As day concedes, the night we weave.
On blankets white, the world aglow,
A shimmering dance begins to flow.

Stars emerge in the chilly air,
Whispers of dusk, a tender care.
Moonlight drapes on the snow-kissed ground,
In every shimmer, beauty's found.

Crickets hush in the fading light,
Hearts entwine in the quiet night.
As dreams take flight on winds so free,
We find our place, just you and me.

Distant Echoes of Frost

Through the trees, whispers sigh,
A chill wraps around, night draws nigh.
Stars shimmer in the icy air,
Memories linger, with time to spare.

Footsteps crunch on powdered ground,
Silent moments, peace profound.
Each flake falls, a soft refrain,
In the stillness, echoes remain.

Enchanted by Pure Serenity

Moonlit skies, a silver gleam,
Whispers flow as if a dream.
Gentle winds, a lover's breath,
In this calm, we dance with death.

Petals drift on quiet streams,
Reflecting all our softest dreams.
Nature's song in every sway,
Enchanted hearts will find their way.

Tidal Waves of Snow Whispers

Snowflakes flutter, soft and light,
Carrying secrets of the night.
Each one twirls like a fleeting thought,
In their embrace, warmth is sought.

A tapestry of white unfolds,
Binding stories that time holds.
Echoes of laughter, lingering near,
In this silence, all is clear.

The Calm Before the Frost

Leaves surrender to the breeze,
Nature pauses, a moment to seize.
The earth holds its breath in suspense,
Awaiting winter's recompense.

Crimson hues fade to gray,
As daylight melts and drifts away.
In twilight's arms, shadows play,
The calm whispers before the fray.

Ethereal Calm of Shimmering Night

Stars whisper secrets to the sky,
Moonlight dances, a gentle sigh.
Cool breezes weave through ancient trees,
Crickets serenade under the eaves.

Shadows linger, soft as a sigh,
Nature's lullaby, a soft reply.
Dreamers glide on the mist of sleep,
In this night, the world seems deep.

The lake reflects a silken glow,
Ripples tell stories only they know.
Time stands still in this twilight hush,
As hearts unfurl in the evening's blush.

Whispers of night in velvet embrace,
Lost in the wonder of this sacred space.
Breath of the cosmos in every heart,
A fleeting moment, pure as art.

Floating on clouds of ethereal bliss,
Wrapped in the magic of love's soft kiss.
As dawn approaches, dreams take flight,
Leaving traces in the shimmering night.

Luminous Dreams Drifting Down

Dewdrops glisten in the moon's soft light,
Waking the world from the depth of night.
Whispers of hope in the gentle breeze,
Carrying secrets through swaying trees.

Stars paint stories across the sky,
Glimmers of dreams where wishes lie.
The dawn peeks in with a blush so bright,
Cradling dreams in the warmth of light.

Clouds drift slowly, a soft white quilt,
Embroidered with dreams that twilight built.
In the stillness, hearts begin to race,
As morning kisses the dark's embrace.

Echoes of laughter in the waking morn,
Innocent pleasures, like roses reborn.
With every heartbeat, the day unfolds,
And luminous dreams turn to stories told.

In the glow of day, we chase and seek,
Finding solace in moments unique.
Though dreams may fade with the sun's bright crown,
Hope remains—luminous, drifting down.

Illumination Under the Frozen Veil

In shadows deep, the lanterns glow,
Whispers of warmth in the chilling snow.
A frost-kissed world, each breath a cloud,
Starlight weaves soft, a shimmering shroud.

Branches heavy, with crystals adorned,
Secrets of winter, in silence, are sworn.
Glimmers of hope in the starry night,
Hearts entwined in the frozen light.

The Shimmering Quiet of Evening White

Gentle snowflakes dance through the air,
A symphony of silence, beyond compare.
Each flake unique, a delicate grace,
In the twilight hush, time finds its place.

The moon casts silver on blankets wide,
A tranquil canvas where dreams abide.
Whispers of winter lull the day,
As shadows stretch and softly sway.

Frost and Light in a Frozen Waltz

Twilight drapes its frosty embrace,
Nature sways in a delicate pace.
Lights twinkle like stars on the ground,
A frozen ballet in silence found.

Chill fills the air, yet warmth persists,
In every heartbeat, winter insists.
The earth wears white, a regal gown,
As twilight spins her soft, silver crown.

Celestial Veils of a Winter's Dream

Stars alight in the velvet sky,
Each twinkle tells a lullaby.
Winter's breath softly sings along,
In the heart of night, a gentle song.

Veils of snow wrap the world in peace,
A moment paused, where worries cease.
Under the cosmos, spirits rise,
Entwined in magic, under cold skies.

Illuminated Drift of the Night

Stars above softly glimmer,
Whispers of shadows entwine,
Moonlight dances on waters,
As dreams in silence align.

Night's embrace wraps around,
Casting a spell so divine,
Every heartbeat resounds,
In this realm, hearts combine.

Soft breezes carry secrets,
Through the trees they will glide,
In the hush of the darkness,
Our hopes and fears coincide.

Waves of tranquility flow,
A canopy woven tight,
Under stars' watchful eye,
We drift in endless night.

Echoes of laughter linger,
Beneath the shimmering light,
In dreams we are united,
In this illuminated night.

Frost-Kissed Echoes of Twilight

The day fades in blush and gold,
As silence blankets the ground,
Frost-tinged whispers unfold,
Echoes of twilight profound.

Crystal patterns weave and trace,
Nature's artistry unveiled,
In the stillness we embrace,
Where time gently exhaled.

Each breath is a fleeting mist,
Caught in the chill of the air,
Beauty in moments we've kissed,
In twilight's gentle flair.

Beneath the vast sapphire sky,
Our spirits begin to soar,
With each glance, we quietly sigh,
As the evening bids us explore.

Frost-kissed echoes invite,
Moments lost, forever near,
Cradled in the fading light,
These treasures we hold dear.

Mystical Light on Winter's Breath

As night drapes its velvet cloak,
Mystical lights begin to glow,
Painting shadows with every stroke,
While winter's breath whispers low.

Each flake of snow's a story,
Adorning branches all around,
In this serene, close glory,
Magic on the frozen ground.

The world hushed in silver whispers,
A blanket soft, widely cast,
Heartbeats synchronize like drifters,
In a landscape unsurpassed.

Crystalline lanterns softly gleam,
Beneath the cold, radiant sky,
In the winter's enchanting dream,
We find ourselves drifting high.

Mystical light guides our way,
Through this tapestry so bright,
In winter's embrace we sway,
Wrapped in the calm of night.

A Frosted Symphony of Stillness

In stillness wrapped by the dawn,
Nature pauses, breath held tight,
Frosted symphony is drawn,
In the cradle of soft light.

Branches wear a shimmering veil,
Each moment a note in time,
The silence tells an old tale,
In harmony's gentle rhyme.

Whispers of breezes entwine,
Carrying secrets untold,
A symphonic blend divine,
Where warmth meets the winter's cold.

As we tread on the crisp ground,
The world feels fresh and anew,
In stillness, peace can be found,
Like a song that rings true.

Join in this frost-kissed display,
Feel the magic unfold here,
A frosted symphony at play,
In silence, the heart draws near.

The Grace of Softly Falling White

Snowflakes dance in quiet skies,
Whispers soft, as daylight dies.
Each one falls, a fleeting dream,
Cloaking earth in silent gleam.

Branches bow with gentle grace,
Nature's art, a pure embrace.
Blankets white on every ground,
A peaceful hush, a timeless sound.

Children laugh, their joy so bright,
Building castles, pure delight.
In this world, the heart finds peace,
As troubles drift, and worries cease.

Moonlight glows on frosty eves,
Sparkling jewels on frozen leaves.
Each moment holds a sacred light,
In the grace of softly falling white.

In the Embrace of Winter's Breath

The world lies wrapped in cold embrace,
As winter whispers, time slows its pace.
Frosted air with every sigh,
A chill that lifts the heart up high.

Pine trees stand in stately line,
Their needles glistening, sharp, and fine.
Snowflakes kiss the earth's soft skin,
A spell that lures the soul within.

Fires crackle, warmth does bloom,
Embers dance within the room.
A world of peace, as shadows play,
In winter's breath, we drift away.

The quiet night, a tranquil friend,
With silver stars that twinkly blend.
In deep embrace, we find our bliss,
In moments shared, love's tender kiss.

Frozen Shimmers of Time

Icicles hang, sharp and bright,
Reflecting shards of morning light.
Time stands still in frozen air,
A pause that feels beyond compare.

Paths of white lead hearts to roam,
In the cold, we find our home.
Footsteps crunching in the night,
Each sound echoes, pure delight.

Stars above, a crystal sky,
Winking softly as we sigh.
Moments trapped, yet fleeting fast,
In frozen shimmers, we are cast.

Breathe in deep the frosty grace,
Time suspended in this place.
As winter weaves its artful line,
We find ourselves in frozen time.

Reflections on a Snow-Covered Silence

The snow-laden branches bow low,
Touching paths we dare to go.
In silence thick, the world awakes,
A broken hush, as stillness takes.

Mirrored calm on every face,
Nature's soft and pure embrace.
Thoughts drift like clouds, pure and white,
In the stillness, hearts take flight.

Gentle flakes, a timeless dance,
In their grace, we find our chance.
Step by step, through glistening light,
Reflections bloom in winter's night.

Each breath a cloud in chilly air,
We pause, we listen, hearts laid bare.
In snow-covered silence, we see,
The beauty of what it means to be.

Frost-Laden Whispers on the Breeze

Whispers soft in chilling air,
Frosty breath on branches bare.
Nature's quilt, a white embrace,
Silent magic, tranquil space.

Footsteps crunch on frosted ground,
Echoes of a world profound.
Each breath fogs the starry night,
In this stillness, all feels right.

Icicles hang like crystal tears,
Frozen tales of winter years.
Every flake a tale untold,
Glints of silver, bright and bold.

Whispers dance on winter's song,
In this wonder, we belong.
Frost-laden air, a sweet caress,
Embraced by nature's cold finesse.

Beneath the moon, the shadows play,
In this beauty, hearts shall stay.
Frost-laden whispers, calm and deep,
In dreams of winter, softly sleep.

The Glimmer of a Winter's Night

Stars ignite the velvet sky,
Frosty breath as shadows sigh.
Moonlight dances on the snow,
In its glow, the world will glow.

Whispers float on chilly air,
Nature wrapped in silver flair.
A blanket soft, a quiet light,
Embracing all this winter night.

Every flake, a diamond's gleam,
Caught within the midnight dream.
Silent wishes take their flight,
Underneath the starry light.

Crystals shimmer, bright and clear,
Winter's wonder gathering near.
Footsteps mark the paths of grace,
In this stillness, find your place.

The world aglow, a frosty kiss,
In each moment, find your bliss.
The glimmer calls, the heart takes flight,
Wrapped in warmth on winter's night.

Reflections of Light on White Abyss

In the stillness, shadows play,
Light refracts in bright array.
Snowflakes dance on gentle breeze,
Whispers soft among the trees.

A canvas pure, a sight divine,
Reflections gleam, the stars align.
Ripples shimmer on the ground,
Silent beauty all around.

Icicles drip like crystal tears,
Holding tightly winter's fears.
Each glimmer sings a lullaby,
In this wonder, dreams can fly.

White abyss, a world aglow,
Through the night, the soft winds blow.
Every sparkle, a fleeting chance,
In this magic, heart's romance.

Reflections of a moment's grace,
In this stillness, find your place.
Light unfolds in every space,
A dance of peace, a soft embrace.

The Lullaby of Glows and Flakes

Whispers float in winter's night,
Gentle glows, a pure delight.
Snowflakes falling, silence near,
Heartfelt echoes, crystal clear.

Each flake spins, a story told,
In the dark, they shimmer bold.
A lullaby of soft refrain,
Wrapping dreams in frosty chain.

The moon's embrace, a gentle kiss,
Fills the night with warmth and bliss.
Underneath this magic's spell,
Winter's tales begin to swell.

Stars above in sparkling rows,
Shine down on the world below.
Each twinkle brings a hope's new chance,
In this glow, a cherished dance.

The lullaby of glows and flakes,
In every heart, the winter wakes.
Embrace the night, let spirits soar,
In this wonder, love restores.

The Stillness of Crystal Nights

Underneath the starry skies,
A hush falls on the land,
Whispers of the moonlit dreams,
Hold the world in gentle hands.

Trees stand tall, a fortress strong,
Glittering in silver light,
Every breath a frozen sigh,
As time drifts softly into night.

Crystals twinkle, pathways gleam,
Footsteps muted, spirits high,
Nature breathes a silent scheme,
In the stillness, shadows lie.

Icicles hang like crystal tears,
A melody of winter's grace,
Each moment vast, unbound by fears,
Eternal in this frozen place.

Seeking warmth in night's embrace,
Gentle sighs of love's delight,
In this tranquil, sacred space,
We dance beneath the shimmering light.

Echoes in the Snowdrift

A soft layer blankets the ground,
Whispers of the frosty air,
Echoes linger all around,
A memory, tender and rare.

Footprints tell a silent tale,
Wanderers mark their paths anew,
In each flake, a dream, a veil,
Of hope and joy, fresh as dew.

Branches heavy with snowy lace,
Curve and bend with winter's might,
In this serene and quiet place,
Time flows like the softest light.

Children laughing, hearts ablaze,
Rolling finding joy in play,
As snowflakes dance in a swirl craze,
They beckon life, come what may.

The world hushes, pauses now,
For nature's song, so pure, so bright,
In every drift and every bough,
Echoes linger through the night.

Shadows of a Frozen Dawn

As daybreak spills its golden hue,
The chill wraps 'round the silent trees,
Shadows dance where light breaks through,
A tranquil breath upon the breeze.

Breath of frost upon my skin,
The world awakens, pure and new,
Within the stillness, warmth within,
A symphony of colors bloom.

Crimson skies meet icy blue,
A canvas painted, bold and bright,
In every shadow, hope renewed,
As dreams embrace the morning light.

Birds take flight, a joyous song,
Nature's choir sings along,
In the quiet, we belong,
To the rhythm, soft and strong.

With every heartbeat, dawn is drawn,
A promise held in morning's grace,
As shadows dance, the night is gone,
Reveling in this warm embrace.

Lullaby of the White Blankets

A quilt of snow wraps the land tight,
Whispers lull the restless hearts,
In this haven, soft and bright,
Peace descends as daylight departs.

The moon sings softly from above,
Casting dreams on frozen streams,
Each flake carries warmth and love,
Cradling hopes in gentle beams.

Winter's breath, a soothing balm,
Tucks the world in quiet grace,
Every moment, still and calm,
In the night's warm, soft embrace.

Stars blink like eyes, a tender gaze,
Watching over slumbering souls,
While nature hums its softest praise,
In this cradle, joy consoles.

So let the winds weave sweet delight,
A lullaby of snow's caress,
In the stillness of the night,
We find our peace, our happiness.

Whispers of Frosted Dreams

In the hush of twilight's grasp,
Frosted whispers softly creep,
Dreams weave through the silver light,
As the world begins to sleep.

Beneath the stars, a tapestry,
Stitched by night's gentle hand,
Silent wishes float like clouds,
Across a slumbering land.

Branches draped in crystal veils,
Sparkling like a hidden gem,
Each breath a frosty echo,
In this enchanted realm.

Voices carried on the breeze,
Soft as lullabies unfold,
A serenade of icy dreams,
In the winter's chilly hold.

Time stands still, a fleeting dance,
Where shadows briefly play,
In whispers of frosted dreams,
Night turns to gentle day.

Veils of Winter's Embrace

Veils of winter wrap the earth,
Softly cloaked in white and grey,
Every flake a lover's touch,
Melting doubts away.

Branches adorned in shimmering lace,
Glisten under a silver hue,
Nature breathes in quiet peace,
As the night bids adieu.

A quiet hush covers all,
Crickets cease their evening song,
In the calm, an echo calls,
Where heartbeats still belong.

Embers glow in hearth's warm light,
Casting shadows soft and long,
Wrapped in winter's sweet embrace,
Together, we are strong.

With every step on crunching snow,
A tale of love unfolds,
In veils of winter's embrace,
A story to be told.

Glistening Tranquility

Glistening under twilight's eye,
The world is painted in soft light,
Each shard of ice, a diamond clear,
Reflecting dreams that take flight.

A gentle breeze whispers by,
Carrying glimpses of delight,
Nature's canvas, so serene,
In the stillness of the night.

Snowflakes dance like fairies bright,
In their waltz, a pure ballet,
Every movement sparks a smile,
As the skies begin to sway.

Amidst the chill, warmth lingers near,
In the heart, a quiet peace,
Glistening tranquility found,
In love's sweet, soft release.

The night stretches, vast and clear,
Wrapped in dreams, we find our breath,
In glistening tranquility,
We embrace the night, not death.

Moonlight Kissing the Snow

Moonlight spills on snow-kissed ground,
Wrapping all in silvery folds,
Whispers of the night abound,
In secrets that it holds.

Stars above like diamonds bright,
Blink in gentle, rhythmic flow,
In the calm of winter's night,
Moonlight kissing the snow.

Silent shadows softly flirt,
With the breeze that plays along,
While the heartbeats intertwine,
In a rhythm, sweet and strong.

Each footprint softly leaves its mark,
In this dreamscape, pure and slow,
With every step, a love ignites,
As moonlight kisses the snow.

Together, we find our way,
Through the night, hand in hand,
In the light of dreams fulfilled,
In this softly frozen land.

Muffled Footsteps in Crystal

In the stillness, shadows creep,
Whispers of the night, so deep.
Footprints vanish, soft as sighs,
Beneath the stars, the silence lies.

Frosted branches, glistening bright,
Underneath the pale moonlight.
Lost in echoes of the past,
Where time and memory hold fast.

A breathless hush, the world at peace,
Nature's beauty, never cease.
Each step taken, carefully planned,
In a wonderland so grand.

Frozen laughter fills the air,
Dancing lightly without a care.
The night unfolds its quiet charms,
Embraced within the winter's arms.

As dawn approaches, shadows flee,
Muffled footsteps set them free.
A fleeting moment, gone too soon,
Underneath the watchful moon.

Secrets Beneath the Snowy Veil

Beneath the snow, a secret sleeps,
Whispers hidden, nature keeps.
Silent truths in layers deep,
Awake in dreams, where stillness sweeps.

The world transformed, a canvas white,
Tales of mystery, out of sight.
Winds carry stories, soft and low,
Woven in a shroud of snow.

What lies buried in the frost?
Memories cherished, never lost.
Each flake a promise, pure and true,
Unveiling secrets, old and new.

In quiet moments, listen close,
The earth holds wonders, it engross.
Softly falling, time unravels fast,
Echoes of the winter past.

As night descends with icy breath,
The snowy veil conceals its depth.
Yet in the still, we find a way,
To glimpse the truths that softly lay.

Moonbeams on a Frozen Canvas

On a canvas of ice, moonlight dances,
Casting dreams in silver chances.
Shimmers glow, a magical sight,
Painting shadows within the night.

Each crystal spark, a tale untold,
In winter's grasp, both soft and bold.
Beneath the gaze of the starry swarm,
The world transforms, so quiet, warm.

Footsteps echo, soft and clear,
As moonbeams whisper to those near.
Illuminated paths we trace,
In the beauty found in this place.

Frozen lakes reflect the skies,
Mirroring secrets with soft sighs.
Underneath the chill, hearts ignite,
Bathed in the glow of the night.

Nature's soft brush, a fleeting art,
Capturing moments that fill the heart.
In every glow, a story we weave,
Through moonlit nights, we dare believe.

Dreamlike Winter Reveries

In dreamlike hues, the world unfolds,
Winter tales that silence holds.
Frosted whispers in the air,
Guiding thoughts beyond despair.

Gentle snowflakes drift and twirl,
Each one a wish, a shimm'ring pearl.
In this stillness, hopes reside,
As magic lingers, deep inside.

Eyes closed tight, the heart takes flight,
Imagining wonders of the night.
Fairy tales in the frosted glow,
A realm where only dreamers go.

Lullabies in the evening chill,
As the world beneath the snow, stands still.
In the depths of winter's embrace,
We find ourselves in this tranquil space.

Awakened hearts, through snow we roam,
In the stillness, we find home.
Each breath a promise, softly spun,
In the dreamscape where we run.

The Magic of Hushed Landscapes

In whispers soft, the breezes play,
Beneath the trees, where shadows sway.
A tranquil hue paints all around,
In nature's arms, peace can be found.

The hills embrace the fading light,
As stars emerge, igniting night.
With every glance, a story wakes,
In golden fields, our heart just aches.

Silent paths through emerald glades,
Where secrets dwell, and time cascades.
Each step we take, a sacred vow,
To cherish now, this quiet how.

The rivers hum a gentle tune,
Under the gaze of silver moon.
A place where dreams and silence blend,
In hushed landscapes, our spirits mend.

With every breath, the magic grows,
In nature's arms, where wonder flows.
These sacred scenes, forever etched,
In memory's heart, forever stretched.

Frost-kissed Reflections

Winter's breath on crystal streams,
Where sunlight fades, and silence gleams.
Soft flakes dance in the chilly air,
A quilt of white, beyond compare.

Trees stand still, in frosted grace,
Nature's mirror, a tranquil space.
Each twig adorned with icy lace,
A captivating, silent embrace.

Footprints fade in the softest snow,
Where shadows linger, calm and low.
The world transformed, in white attire,
Awakens souls with quiet fire.

Reflections glimmer, still and bright,
Where day surrenders softly to night.
In winter's charm, we find our peace,
A fleeting moment, a sweet release.

Beneath the stars, a canvas fair,
Frost-kissed dreams hang in the air.
In tender whispers, night takes flight,
As nature bids us soft goodnight.

Chasing the Glistening Silence

Amid the woods, where stillness lies,
In glistening hues, the world complies.
Captured breaths, in frosty air,
Moments lost, beyond compare.

Soft echoes drift between the trees,
Where time stands still, like gentle breeze.
With every step, the silence grows,
In nature's fold, where stillness flows.

Reflections shimmer on frozen streams,
Engulfed in peace, we drift in dreams.
Each whisper soft, each glance refined,
A sacred bond, our souls aligned.

We chase the calm, the light, the grace,
Through hidden paths and quiet space.
In glistening silence, hearts unite,
With echoed joys in soft twilight.

At day's end, when shadows pause,
We gather calm and sweet applause.
In nature's arms, we find our way,
In glistening silence, we will stay.

Elegant Stillness in White

Softly falls the tender snow,
Blanketing the earth below.
A stillness lingers in the air,
As nature weaves her artistry rare.

Each flake a whisper, light and sweet,
Transforming paths beneath our feet.
With every breath, a slumbered sigh,
In white-clad splendor, dreams can fly.

Frosted branches, a delicate lace,
Adorn the trees with timeless grace.
Beneath the sky, a canvas bright,
An elegant stillness, pure delight.

In quiet realms where shadows play,
A symphony of white ballet.
Each flurry dances, fleeting, free,
In tranquil moments, just to be.

As daylight fades, the stars ignite,
In elegant stillness, hearts take flight.
A peaceful hush binds day to night,
In whispered dreams, we hold on tight.

Dreaming in a Frosty Light

In the hush of winter nights,
Stars twinkle like distant lights.
A blanket white covers the ground,
In this stillness, dreams are found.

Whispers of cold drift through the air,
A frosty breath, a moment rare.
Moonlight dances on frozen lakes,
Each step careful, as the stillness wakes.

Trees adorned in crystalline lace,
Nature's art, a tranquil space.
Silence wraps the world in peace,
In this magic, all worries cease.

Frosted windows, soft and bright,
Reflect the wonders of the night.
In this moment, we embrace,
The beauty found in winter's grace.

Dreaming softly in a frost's embrace,
Time stands still in this serene place.
A canvas painted with stars so fine,
In the frosty light, our spirits shine.

Choreography of Light and Snow

In the dance of night and day,
Snowflakes swirl and drift away.
Silver sparkles fill the air,
Nature's art, beyond compare.

Each flake spins in a gentle waltz,
Creating patterns, no faults.
Moonbeams cast a soft embrace,
In this ballet, a loving grace.

Whispers of wind join the show,
Guiding the flakes, to and fro.
A glimmer here, a shimmer there,
In this moment, hearts lay bare.

Footprints trace a rhythmic path,
In this world, we feel the math.
Nature's numbers, pure and true,
In every flake, a dance anew.

As dawn breaks with golden light,
The choreography takes flight.
In the silence after the glow,
We cherish winter's sweet tableau.

Glittering Stillness of Frosted Horizon

Beyond the hills, the frost does cling,
A shimmering hush, the stillness sings.
With every breath, the chill unfolds,
A story of winter, gently told.

Frosted branches reach for the sky,
In a world where time seems to fly.
Light glitters soft on every crest,
In this silence, we find our rest.

The horizon stretches, vast and wide,
Frost-wrapped dreams in the countryside.
A blanket of white, both calm and bright,
Guides us home in the fading light.

Each glint a promise, a spark of hope,
In the quiet, we learn to cope.
Here in the frost, embrace the peace,
In stillness, our souls find release.

Beneath the stars, the world is meek,
A frosted horizon, forever unique.
In this calm, we find our way,
Guided by the light of a winter's day.

Enchanted Glow in the Frigid Air

In the night where shadows play,
A glow emerges, soft and gay.
Frigid air wraps around tight,
Yet warmth shines in the heart's light.

Whispers of frost kiss the ground,
In this beauty, magic is found.
Stars sparkle in twilight's embrace,
Casting hope in this frozen space.

With every breath, a gentle mist,
In the air, fairy tales twist.
A lantern's flicker, a kindled flame,
Fills the darkness, calling our name.

Nature's canvas, a tapestry bright,
Painted with dreams in the still of the night.
Each moment a gift, a story to share,
In our hearts, the enchanted air.

So let us wander through this glow,
In the frosty depths, let our spirits flow.
Embracing the chill, with laughter and cheer,
In the frigid air, we have nothing to fear.

A Hushed Symphony of Ice

In silence deep, the ice does sing,
A shiver here, a crystal ring.
Beneath the frost, the whispers dwell,
Nature's secret, a frozen spell.

Each breath a note, distinct and clear,
The world in white, no need for cheer.
A symphony composed of chill,
Where quietude and wonder fill.

Glimmering shards in moonlit glow,
The night's embrace, a soft tableau.
Every step, the crunching sound,
In this realm, peace is found.

With every flake, a note is played,
In harmony, the night invades.
The cold caress, a gentle guide,
In this frozen song, we abide.

The final bow, the dawn arrives,
With warming sun, the stillness thrives.
Yet in our hearts, the music stays,
A hushed symphony of icy ways.

When Stars Meet Frost

Above the world, the stars ignite,
As frost descends, a wondrous sight.
Celestial gleam on icy ground,
In this moment, peace is found.

Whispers of night in the silver air,
Infinite wonders, beyond compare.
Moonbeams dance on a frosty sheet,
Where earth and sky in silence meet.

Each twinkle holds a frozen dream,
In winter's grasp, all things redeem.
A tapestry woven, bright and bold,
In chilly hands, warm tales are told.

The breath of night, a gentle sigh,
While stars and frost in stillness lie.
A fleeting moment, forever stitched,
In nature's book, our hearts are licked.

So let us pause, in awe we stand,
When stars meet frost, hand in hand.
The beauty found in silence deep,
A memory forever to keep.

Snowflakes on a Whispered Breeze

Softly they fall, the snowflakes sweet,
Like whispers shared, they glide and meet.
Each flake a story, unique and bright,
Dancing through the gentle light.

A twirling waltz upon the air,
Carried gently, without a care.
In winter's arms, they twirl and spin,
A fleeting grace, where dreams begin.

Nature's laughter in every drift,
A moment's pause, the perfect gift.
They blanket earth in soft embrace,
Transforming all in winter's grace.

The world adorned in shimmering white,
As snowflakes whisper through the night.
A peace descends, so pure, so fine,
In every flake, a spark divine.

As dawn awakens, light starts to gleam,
The snowflakes dance, a living dream.
In memories kept, they find their flight,
Whispers of beauty, pure delight.

Clouds Wrapped in Winter's Touch

Clouds drift soft in a silver haze,
Wrapped in winter's gentle ways.
A shroud of white, they float and roam,
Embracing earth, a cozy home.

With every breath, the chill we kiss,
A quiet spell, a frosty bliss.
The world below waits in repose,
As nature's art begins to pose.

They paint the sky in shades of gray,
A canvas vast where dreams can play.
With whispers low, they start to weep,
A tender gift from heights so deep.

Each drop a promise, every flake,
Brings life anew, where dreams awake.
In winter's grasp, the clouds bestow,
A biting coolness, and then the glow.

So linger here, beneath their shade,
In winter's touch, our fears do fade.
For in their fold, we softly lie,
Wrapped in warmth, as life floats by.

Frosted Serenity

In the quiet of dawn's embrace,
Snowflakes gracefully trace.
Whispers of chill air's song,
Nature's peace, where we belong.

Branches draped in silvery frost,
All the warmth of summer lost.
A stillness that softly calls,
Echoing through pine-clad halls.

Footprints soften on the ground,
Magic in silence found.
Each breath becomes a cloud,
In solitude, we are proud.

Crystals dance upon the lake,
A mirror where dreamers wake.
Time slows down its furious pace,
Holding moments in gentle grace.

As twilight wraps the world in white,
Stars emerge, sparkling bright.
In this frosted serenity,
We find our shared eternity.

The Dance of Winter's Veil

Snowflakes twirl like dancers fair,
Graceful movements fill the air.
Upon the stage of frozen ground,
Winter's beauty, profound.

The chill awakens hearts anew,
With each flurry, sights in view.
Nature dons her crystal gown,
In this silence, we won't drown.

Branches sway with gentle sighs,
Underneath the slate gray skies.
Whispers of the frosty breeze,
Bringing calm, inviting ease.

Candlelight glimmers in the night,
Against the white, a warm delight.
Families gather close and near,
Surrounded by love's cheer.

In the dance of winter's veil,
Magic flutters without fail.
Lost in wonder, we will stay,
While snowflakes dance, come what may.

Beneath the Quiet Flurry

Beneath the quiet flurry's sway,
Life takes on a softer play.
Whispers carried on the breeze,
Nature's symphony to ease.

Fields of white stretch far and wide,
A peaceful hush we cannot hide.
Footprints fading, stories told,
In shimmering blankets of purest gold.

Robins nest in frosty trees,
While silence wraps the world with ease.
Echoes of laughter fill the air,
As joy is found everywhere.

Moonlight bathes the scene in grace,
A gentle warmth in winter's space.
Here we breathe, we laugh, we sigh,
Together under the whispering sky.

Beneath the tranquil, swirling snow,
Hearts unite, and spirits flow.
In this stillness, we shall thrive,
For in this peace, we come alive.

Embracing the Polar Stillness

In the hush of polar night,
Stars ignite the sky's delight.
Chills wrap round like tender arms,
Nature's beauty, full of charms.

Whispers weave through frosty air,
Each breath a cloud, light and rare.
Silence reigns where shadows play,
In this stillness, we shall stay.

Icicles hang with frozen grace,
Reflecting time and empty space.
Footsteps echo, soft and light,
Held within the winter's bite.

Gathered close by fire's glow,
Hearts entwined, feelings grow.
In this embrace of night and chill,
Joy ignites with every thrill.

As dawn unfurls her icy hue,
Awakening skies in sparkling blue.
We hold the stillness close and dear,
In winter's embrace, love's crystal clear.

Secrets of a Frosted Night

In the embrace of silent chill,
Moonlight whispers soft and low.
Snowflakes dance with quiet thrill,
Painting dreams where shadows grow.

Stars peek through the velvet dark,
Glimmers of the world unseen.
Echoes of a hidden spark,
Calling forth the night's serene.

Breath of winter, crisp and clear,
Carving paths on frosted ground.
Every secret held so near,
In the stillness, truth is found.

Trees adorned with icy lace,
Nature dons a regal guise.
In this frozen, timeless space,
Sorrows fade, and beauty lies.

Whispers linger, softly hum,
Memories in flurries swirl.
In this night, the heartbeats drum,
As the frost begins to twirl.

Illuminated Drift in Stillness

Amid the hush of soft twilight,
Glimmers dance on snowy plains.
Moonbeams weave a silver light,
Carving dreams from crystal chains.

Whispers rise like gentle gusts,
Carrying the tales of yore.
Frozen moments, melted trust,
Speak of wonders to explore.

In the stillness, voices rest,
Echoes of the past remain.
Every heartbeat, every quest,
Fades into the amber grain.

Stars ignite the vast expanse,
Casting spells of silent grace.
In this tranquil, sweet romance,
Time and space embrace with pace.

Illuminated veils unfurl,
Each breath whispers, softly shared.
In this drift, the heartbeats whirl,
As the frosted night has dared.

A Chorus of Frosted Stars

In the night, where silence reigns,
Frosted stars begin to sing.
Melodies in icy chains,
Echoing the love they bring.

Every twinkle, softly cast,
Tales of joy, of pain, of loss.
In their glow, all shadows past,
Illuminate what hearts emboss.

A chorus rises with the dawn,
Filling spaces once so bare.
As the cold begins to yawn,
Each note drifts upon the air.

Whispers of a winter's night,
Swaying under moonlit skies.
In their dance, a pure delight,
Where the endless magic lies.

Frosted stars, a guiding light,
Lead the way through darkened roads.
In their warmth, all feels right,
Carrying our heavy loads.

Veils of Quiet Brightness

Draped in soft, ethereal glow,
Morning light begins to creep.
Veils of quiet beauty flow,
Lifting dreams from gentle sleep.

In this soft and tender space,
Nature breathes, awake anew.
Every shadow finds its place,
In the warmth of brightening hue.

Birds take flight with morning's call,
Painting skies with joyful song.
While the winter's grip may stall,
Hope and light will linger long.

With each ray, the ice will melt,
In the heart where love ignites.
Fleeting moments gently felt,
In the hush of frosted nights.

Veils of quiet brightness spin,
Wrapping all in pure embrace.
As a new day stirs within,
Life begins its gentle race.

Nature's Hushed White Symphony

Snowflakes fall on silent ground,
Whispers of winter all around.
Trees wear blankets, pure and white,
Nature sings in soft twilight.

Frozen streams in gentle flow,
A tranquil scene, a quiet show.
Footprints left, a fleeting trace,
In this calm, I find my place.

Frosty air, a breath so crisp,
In this beauty, I cannot resist.
Hushed the world, as dreams take flight,
Wrapped in nature's pure delight.

Stars emerge in velvet skies,
Moonlight dances, softly lies.
In this moment, all feels right,
Nature's hush, a sweet respite.

Each flake tells a story old,
Nature's art, a sight to behold.
In winter's grasp, hearts ignite,
In the hush, we take our flight.

The Hibernate of Shimmering Light

Glowing embers in the night,
Dreams suspended in soft light.
The world slows, a gentle sigh,
Time stands still, as stars reply.

Cloaked in warmth, we drift away,
In quiet shadows, spirits play.
Frosty windows, patterns bright,
Whispers fill the cool, crisp night.

Candles flicker, shadows dance,
In this stillness, take a chance.
Let the light guide through the dark,
A shimmering path, a hopeful spark.

Winter's breath on skin so kind,
Moments lost in heart and mind.
Through the cold, we find our way,
In shimmering light, we choose to stay.

As the world outside sleeps tight,
We embrace this pure delight.
In hibernation's soft embrace,
We find beauty in this space.

Cloaked in Soft Embrace

Winter whispers, the world at peace,
Gentle winds bring soft release.
Nature wraps in frosty lace,
A quiet hug, a warm embrace.

Branches bare against the grey,
Silent rhythms lead the way.
Blanketed hills, a soft retreat,
In this stillness, hearts compete.

The moonlight casts a silver glow,
Painting shadows, soft and slow.
Frosted fields like dreams unfold,
In this silence, tales are told.

Each breath a cloud, each step a song,
In this embrace, we all belong.
Nature cradles, safe and sound,
In the hush, true peace is found.

Cloaked in warmth, we linger long,
In winter's charm, we grow strong.
Every moment, sweet and rare,
Wrapped in love, beyond compare.

The Poetry of a Winter's Night

Silent stars in the velvet sky,
Whispers of dreams as we pass by.
The chill in the air, a gentle kiss,
A winter's night, a moment of bliss.

Snowflakes falling, a soft ballet,
Dancing lightly, then fade away.
Underneath a blanket white,
Nature's canvas gleams with light.

Crackling fires, shadows play,
In cozy homes where hearts can stay.
Stories told with laughter bright,
This is the magic of winter's night.

Stars above like wishes fair,
Each a promise, floating in air.
In this beauty, we find delight,
In the poetry of this night.

Calm descends as dreams take flight,
Wrapped in warmth, holding tight.
The world outside whispers low,
In winter's embrace, we dare to glow.

Pale Luminance on the Frosted Ground

Beneath the pale, a soft glow shines,
Crystals glisten, like fragile lines.
Whispers of winter, gently found,
A tender light on frosted ground.

The trees stand quiet, dressed in white,
Each branch holds dreams, pure and bright.
The world transforms, a soft embrace,
In this serene and wondrous place.

Footsteps crunch on the sparkling crust,
Every step echoes, in frost we trust.
A breath of cold, crisp and clear,
Nature's canvas, drawing near.

As shadows dance in fading light,
The stars awaken, one by one,
Illuminating the frosted white,
A silent spell has just begun.

In this stillness, a heartbeat's pause,
Moments drift without a cause.
With each whisper of the night,
Pale luminance brings delight.

The Quiet Ballet of Winter's Hold

Snowflakes flutter in the air,
Dancing softly, without a care.
Nature's stage, so pure and bright,
The quiet ballet of winter's night.

Each flake a twirl, so unique,
Whispers of beauty, calm and sleek.
In the hush, a tale unfolds,
Of winter's grace, quiet and bold.

Moonlight casts a silver sheen,
Over landscapes painted serene.
Footprints weave a soft refrain,
In the stillness, joy remains.

Frosted breath in the chilly air,
A fleeting moment, captured rare.
In the quiet, hearts take flight,
Ballet of winter, pure delight.

As time stands still in twilight's glow,
Nature whispers secrets low.
With every twirl, a silent tale,
In winter's hold, love will prevail.

Enchanted Whispers Beneath the Flakes

Beneath the flakes, a world concealed,
Magic whispers, gently revealed.
As soft as dreams, the silence flows,
In enchanted realms, where wonder grows.

The night hums low, a soothing sound,
With every flake, new joys abound.
Footsteps dance in a snowy trance,
Each heart awakens to winter's chance.

The trees, they sway with tales untold,
In their embrace, the magic unfolds.
Crystals glimmer in the soft glow,
A wondrous secret the night will show.

Here in the stillness, lost in thought,
Each moment cherished, deeply sought.
Whispers linger, floating free,
Beneath the flakes, a tapestry.

As dawn approaches with golden light,
The world awakens from the night.
Yet in our hearts, the magic stays,
Enchanted whispers, through our days.

Shimmering Whispers on a Chilled Canvas

On a chilled canvas, still and white,
Whispers shimmer, reflecting light.
Nature paints with a delicate brush,
In this moment, there's a hush.

Treetops twinkle with frost-kissed care,
Each branch a story, beyond compare.
Footprints trail where silence reigns,
In frozen dreams, no one remains.

The air is crisp, filled with delight,
As shadows stretch in fading light.
A tranquil scene, with whispers clear,
Calling softly, come linger here.

In every flake lies a promise bright,
A fleeting kiss from the winter night.
With every breath, feel the chill embrace,
Shimmering whispers, a sacred space.

As the dusk wraps the world in grace,
We find our place in this quiet space.
Chilled canvas holds our dreams anew,
Under a sky that sparkles true.

A Frosty Reverie Under Stars

Beneath the canvas of night's veil,
Stars whisper secrets, soft and pale.
Frost-kissed dreams dance upon the ground,
In silent reverie, peace is found.

Moonlight drapes the trees in silver sheets,
Crystalline beauty, where the stillness meets.
With every twinkle, a story unfolds,
Of winter's magic and legends told.

Each breath released, a misty sigh,
As frosty winds through the pines reply.
In this moment, the world feels wide,
Wrapped in wonder, where hearts abide.

The night deepens, a blanket of dreams,
Where laughter echoes and starlight beams.
Time stands still under the celestial dome,
In a frosty reverie, I am home.

In hues of blue, the shadows blend,
A wistful journey where night won't end.
With stars as guides, our spirits soar,
In this frosty realm, forevermore.

Murmurs of Light in the Icy Embrace

In the grip of night, soft whispers rise,
Murmurs of light paint across the skies.
Each glimmer sparkles in the frosty air,
A symphony of silence, pure and rare.

The world is wrapped in an icy embrace,
Crystal tendrils weave through time and space.
Shadows flicker where the moonlight spills,
Crafting a canvas that the heart fulfills.

Beneath the stars, dreams are reborn,
Carried on wings of a winter's morn.
The trees stand tall, dressed in white,
Guardians of secrets hidden from sight.

With every breath, the cold bites sweet,
Nature's lullaby, a heart's gentle beat.
In this realm of frost, we lose our way,
But find our hearts where shadows play.

Echoes of laughter drift through the night,
A melody woven with twinkling light.
In the icy embrace, we find our song,
A journey of whispers, where we belong.

Dusk's Embrace in Crystalline Silence

As dusk descends, the world ignites,
A tapestry woven in fading lights.
Crystalline silence blankets the night,
Wrapping our souls in warmth, so bright.

The air is thick with winter's breath,
Whispers carry tales of life and death.
In this glow, our worries fade,
Lost in the stillness, dreams cascade.

Frosted branches sway, a gentle dance,
In this quiet moment, we take a chance.
To listen closely to the night's refrain,
As stars awaken, a sparkling chain.

Dusk's embrace holds us tight,
Cradling dreams in the soothing flight.
With every heartbeat, the cosmos sings,
Of fragile beauty and wondrous things.

In crystalline silence, we find our way,
A journey marked by night and day.
As the world around us softly glows,
In dusk's embrace, our love just grows.

A Silent Waltz of Radiance and Snow

In the hush of night, the snowflakes twirl,
A silent waltz in a wondrous swirl.
Each flake a whisper, soft as a sigh,
Dancing through moonlight, soaring high.

Radiance glimmers on the silent ground,
A blanket of white where dreams abound.
Footprints follow paths of scattered stars,
Mapping journeys near and far.

In this stillness, hearts intertwine,
Lost in the magic, pure and divine.
With every step on this crystal stage,
We craft our story, turn the page.

The night unfolds, a cherished song,
Where right feels right and wrong feels wrong.
In every breath, a promise we make,
To cherish this moment, for love's sake.

As dawn approaches, the shadows wane,
Transforming the quiet into beauty's reign.
With a silent waltz, we find our way,
In the embrace of the snow, we stay.

Frosted Footsteps in Solitude

In shadows cast by winter's glow,
Soft whispers weave through fields of snow.
Each step a tale in silence told,
Where nature's breath turns bold and cold.

Beneath the trees with branches bare,
A quiet peace hangs in the air.
Footprints linger, fading slow,
As echoes of the past bestow.

The world is hushed, a velvet night,
Stars like diamonds, crisp and bright.
In solitude, the heartbeats rhyme,
With time suspended, still as mime.

Frosted whispers kiss the ground,
Secrets in the frost abound.
Each breath a cloud that fades away,
In winter's grasp where shadows play.

So walk with me through silver light,
In frosted footsteps, pure delight.
Together we shall trace the skies,
In solitude where silence lies.

A Luminous Silence Above

Stars reveal their glimmering dance,
In the stillness, hearts entranced.
The night unfolds a soft embrace,
In luminous silence, time finds space.

Moonlight spills on frozen streams,
Casting shadows, chasing dreams.
Whispers float on crisp night air,
A quiet prayer, a wished despair.

Glistening frost on every bough,
Nature's art, serene somehow.
The world asleep, a gentle sigh,
Underneath the vast, starry sky.

Each gentle breeze, a lullaby,
In this moment, we can fly.
Let worries melt in nighttime's charm,
In silence wrapped, we are kept warm.

So hold my hand beneath the light,
Where calm prevails and dreams ignite.
In a luminous silence above,
We find our peace, our endless love.

Harmonics of Winter Stillness

A symphony of silent nights,
Where every star ignites delights.
The chill of air, a sweet refrain,
In harmonics, peace will reign.

Each flake that falls, a note so pure,
Crafting melodies that endure.
With every breath, a song unfolds,
In winter's grasp, a tale retold.

Branches bow with heavy lace,
Nature's quiet, a soothing grace.
Amidst the still, we feel the pull,
Of winter's voice, serene and full.

A distant echo through the trees,
In breathless hush, a gentle breeze.
Notes of the night, both soft and clear,
Harmonics whisper, come draw near.

So let us dance beneath the moon,
In rhythms soft, our hearts in tune.
In winter stillness, hand in hand,
We find our song in this vast land.

Whispers of Winter's Glow

In twilight's breath, the day surrenders,
As winter's veil, the sky engenders.
Softly glows the frosty air,
With whispers wrapped in twilight's care.

The quiet hush defines the scene,
Each gentle flake a silver queen.
The world adorned in icy dreams,
As starlight twinkles, softly beams.

Paths unknown through snowy fields,
In winter's arms, the spirit yields.
With every crunch beneath our feet,
The heart dances to winter's beat.

Embrace the chill, let worries fade,
In every breath, a memory made.
Whispers of glow, a fleeting art,
A winter song that warms the heart.

So here we stand, in awe, aglow,
In whispers soft of winter's flow.
Together, lost in colors bright,
Creating warmth, despite the night.

Luminous Dances in the Frozen Air

In twilight's grasp, the lights do play,
A shimmer bright in cold ballet.
Each glimmer spins, a fleeting chance,
As nature calls, we join the dance.

With twinkling stars that wink and gleam,
We drift through night, like in a dream.
The world a stage, while moonlight beams,
A waltz of snow, in whispered themes.

The icy breath of winter's kiss,
Transforms the dark, a frozen bliss.
With every step, the past aligns,
In frosty air where magic shines.

With every twirl, the silence glows,
While breath like mist in stillness flows.
The echoes weave a tale so bright,
In luminous dances, pure delight.

So let us glide on crystal plains,
Beneath the stars, our joy remains.
In every heart, the warmth we share,
In luminous dances, frozen air.

The Gentle Poetry of Falling Flakes

Softly drifting from the sky,
Each flake a verse, a lullaby.
A quiet hush as blankets fall,
A gentle touch, embracing all.

Upon the earth, a canvas white,
With every flake, the world ignites.
A dance of silence, pure and free,
The poetry of winter's spree.

In whispers crisp, the moments freeze,
As nature pens with graceful ease.
Each flake a word, a soft refrain,
Creating beauty, absent pain.

Look to the skies, let wonder soar,
In falling flakes, we find much more.
A fragile metaphor revealed,
In gentle poetry, hearts can heal.

A fleeting touch, so soft, so sweet,
Each little flake, a tender greet.
With every drift, the world awakes,
In the gentle poetry of falling flakes.

Enveloping Radiance Through the Trees

In golden light, the branches sway,
Embraced by warmth, they greet the day.
Beneath the boughs, where shadows play,
Enveloping radiance leads the way.

With rustling leaves, the whispers fade,
As sunlight filters, softly laid.
A tapestry of green and gold,
Through ancient trunks, the stories told.

In dappled light, the world transforms,
As nature wears its vibrant forms.
The path ahead, a luminous trail,
With each step forward, hearts set sail.

From sturdy roots to soaring heights,
In radiant warmth, the spirit ignites.
With every breath, the world unfolds,
As beauty through the trees enfolds.

So take a moment, pause and see,
The magic born where branches be.
In enveloping radiance, we find,
The pulse of life, forever kind.

Reflective Glow in the Quiet Night

The moon ascends with silver light,
A calm embrace in the quiet night.
Beneath its gaze, the world finds peace,
In reflective glow, all troubles cease.

Stars in chorus, a twinkling show,
Whispers of dreams in the dark below.
The shadows stretch, the stillness deep,
In reflective glow, our secrets keep.

With every breath, the night unfolds,
A story shared, a truth retold.
As hearts align with the stars above,
In the quiet night, we find our love.

In gentle thoughts, the world drifts slow,
Every moment, a soft tableau.
The cool embrace of the evening air,
In reflective glow, beyond compare.

So let us wander through this sight,
In whispered dreams of the quiet night.
With every step, a spark ignites,
In reflective glow, our souls take flight.

Enchanted Radiance of Snow-Clad Peaks

Beneath the azure, peaks arise,
A quilt of white, where silence lies.
Whispers of winds through valleys flow,
In radiant beams, the snows aglow.

Tall firs stand proud, their branches crowned,
In nature's splendor, beauty found.
Each glimmering flake, a treasure rare,
In this frozen realm, beyond compare.

Gentle the hush, it wraps the land,
With every moment, a master's hand.
Crystalline dreams in cold embrace,
In snow-clad peaks, we find our place.

Majestic sights in winter's grace,
Hearts feel the warmth of this still space.
A canvas pure, so softly drawn,
In enchanted radiance, dusk to dawn.

Stillness Wrapped in Frosted Glow

A blanket soft, the world is hushed,
In frosted glow, the daytime blushed.
Trees stand still, with branches bare,
In this quiet, we breathe the air.

Moonlight dances on the pristine ground,
Each shadow flickers, a peace profound.
Footsteps muffled on snowy trails,
In stillness wrapped, the heart unveils.

Stars blink bright in the cosmos' veil,
Guiding the dreams where hopes set sail.
In winter's night, thoughts intertwine,
With whispers soft, life feels divine.

Time slows down beneath the frost,
In tender moments, never lost.
Silence speaks in a language rare,
Wrapped in stillness, without a care.

Ghostly Hues of a Winter's Night

Upon the canvas, shadows creep,
Ghostly hues in silence seep.
The night is draped in veils of white,
As if the stars blink their last light.

Frosted panes reflect the gleam,
From whispering winds, a haunting dream.
Crisp air curls in a soft embrace,
Ghostly hues set the world in place.

Footsteps echo in the chill,
Whispers wander, calm and still.
The moon dons its silver crown,
Guiding spirits as they drown.

Each breath lingers, a frosty sigh,
Painting breath on the starry sky.
In realms of winter, shadows play,
In ghostly hues, we find our way.

A Ballet of Light in Frostbitten Air

Amber lights twinkle in the night,
A ballet of joy, a magical sight.
Frostbitten air, crisp and bright,
In every flake, a dance of delight.

With every turn, the snowflakes spin,
They twirl and swirl, with laughter within.
Stars hover low, the stage is set,
In winter's grip, we won't forget.

The frosty breeze carries the song,
A melody soft, where we belong.
Each step we take, a rhythm we share,
In this waltz of wonder, beyond compare.

As shadows mingle, night takes flight,
A ballet unfolds in the dimming light.
In frostbitten air, our spirits soar,
In a dance eternal, forevermore.

The Enigma of Frosted Shadows

In the silence, shadows creep,
Frosted whispers, secrets keep.
Glimmers dance on twilight's edge,
Nature's beauty, a silent pledge.

Trees wear crowns of icy lace,
Time stands still in this vast space.
Footsteps muffled, all is still,
In frost's embrace, the world a chill.

Moonlight weaves through branches bare,
Each breath a mist in chilly air.
Shadows blend with winter's light,
Enigmas stir the quiet night.

Glistening paths, a treasure's find,
Frozen dreams of a world entwined.
Each corner holds a tale anew,
In scented winds of icy blue.

Wonders found, yet never told,
In frosted shadows, hearts are bold.
Mysteries in the pale moon's glow,
The enigma of the frost below.

Wind's Gentle Kiss on Crystal Dreams

Gentle whispers in the air,
Breathe the magic, softly rare.
Wind's embrace, a tender sigh,
Crystals shimmer, dreams float high.

Dancing snowflakes, pure and bright,
Caressed beneath the moon's soft light.
In the stillness, heartbeats blend,
Nature's lullaby without end.

Each breath a song, a fleeting chill,
As time stands still on winter's hill.
Brush the silence, intertwine,
In this moment, soft divine.

Whirls of frost, a canvas clean,
Painted dreams, a silver sheen.
With every gust, inspiration flows,
In the wind, a tale that grows.

Crystal visions fill the night,
Guided by the stars so bright.
With each kiss from evening's breeze,
Life unfolds like whispered leaves.

Dreams Adrift in White

Blankets of snow enfold the ground,
In silence deep, peace is found.
Dreams adrift, like stars above,
A canvas pure, a world of love.

Each flake a wish, spinning light,
Floating softly, a fleeting sight.
Hushed whispers brush the frozen air,
In winter's grasp, we find our care.

Shadows long in fading light,
Embrace the still of the night.
Footprints lead where spirits wander,
To capture dreams, we softly ponder.

In the quiet, hearts take flight,
Wrapped in dreams, we ignite.
Adrift in white, the world serene,
A canvas brushed in hopes unseen.

Whispers twirl, like dandelion seeds,
Carried forth on gentle leads.
In the realm of winter's grace,
Find the dreams we dare to chase.

The Elegance of Winter's Blanket

In silence, winter's touch appears,
A blanket soft, it calms our fears.
With each flake, a story spun,
Elegance shines as day is done.

Snowflakes dance and swirl around,
Nature's art, a beauty found.
Each curve a sign of grace bestowed,
As distant stars begin to glow.

Quiet stillness, whispers bright,
Blanket stars in velvet night.
Underneath, the earth sleeps deep,
In winter's grace, the world can weep.

Beneath the frost, life awaits,
In nature's arms, the heart reflects.
With every heartbeat, we ignite,
The elegance of this shared night.

Hope entwined with winter's breath,
In stillness, we escape from death.
Wrapped in dreams, our spirits soar,
Embraced by nature's gentle lore.

The Quiet Serenade of Winter's Light

Whispers of frost cling to the air,
Silent echoes of dreams laid bare.
The moonlight's touch so softly glows,
As stars like scattered jewels propose.

Beneath the hush, the world sleeps tight,
Wrapped in a blanket of silver light.
Each flake a note, each breath a song,
In this serene space, we all belong.

Winds weave tales through the chilly night,
Crystals dance in the soft twilight.
Nature's symphony plays on repeat,
A melody pure, gentle and sweet.

Branches adorned with shimmering lace,
In every corner, a sacred place.
This tranquil moment, a gift so rare,
In winter's light, we float on air.

Within this calm, our hearts take flight,
Finding solace in winter's night.
The quiet serenade wraps us tight,
In shadows of peace, we bask in light.

Glistening Hush Above the Pines

A blanket of white covers the ground,
Where whispers of winter softly surround.
Above the pines, the moon shines bright,
Casting a glow through the still of night.

The air is crisp, filled with a charm,
In this frosty world, we find our calm.
With each breath, the silence speaks,
As nature rests, its beauty peaks.

Stars twinkle softly in velvet skies,
In their glow, the universe lies.
A magic spell lingers in the night,
Bathed in serenity, everything feels right.

Branches sway gently, cradling snow,
In this peaceful realm, time moves slow.
With every sigh, the world feels new,
Wrapped in the hush, beneath skies of blue.

Here, in the quiet, our spirits soar,
Caught in the wonder, wanting more.
Glistening hush, a perfect tune,
Echoes of peace beneath the moon.

Ethereal Dance of Shimmering Snow

Falling softly, a delicate sight,
Each flake a dancer in the pale light.
They twirl and whirl on a winter breeze,
Creating a ballet among the trees.

With grace they settle, a pristine show,
Transforming the world in radiant glow.
Whispers of winter in every sway,
In the hush of night, they gently play.

Moonbeams shimmer on the frozen land,
A sparkling canvas, crafted by hand.
In this ethereal realm, dreams take flight,
As hearts awaken to winter's blissful night.

Every drift speaks of stories untold,
Of warmth and magic against the cold.
In the silence, we find our way,
Guided by snowflakes' soft ballet.

Beyond the pines, where shadows rest,
The dance continues, forever blessed.
An ethereal waltz under starry skies,
In shimmering snow, our spirit flies.

Quiet Reflections on a White Canvas

A frost-kissed dawn breaks the silent night,
Over valleys and hills, pure and white.
Each footprint a story, softly laid,
On this canvas of dreams, winter's parade.

Reflections glisten in the pale sun,
Whispers of warmth, where winter's begun.
The world stands still, wrapped in calm,
In every breath, nature's gentle psalm.

Branches adorned with glistening beads,
In this sacred moment, the heart heeds.
A tranquil scene, the eye delights,
In the shadows of day, where peace ignites.

Quiet reflections, moments to treasure,
In winter's embrace, we find our measure.
Thoughts like snowflakes, they drift and sway,
In this serene space, we wish to stay.

With each passing hour, the light will shift,
Painting the world with winter's gift.
Quiet reflections, a soothing balm,
On this white canvas, we find our calm.

Luminous Whispers Among the Drifts

In the soft glow of twilight's embrace,
Shadows dance upon the frosty lace.
Whispers of warmth in the chilly air,
Carried by lanterns, a flickering flare.

Beneath the stars where the snowflakes twirl,
Voices of silence in a gentle swirl.
Each flake falls softly, a secret told,
Wrapped in the magic of winter's gold.

The moon's soft gaze on the drifts below,
Casts silver dreams on the blankets of snow.
A melody lingers in frozen sighs,
As time dances slowly under winter skies.

Footsteps sound faint on the icy ground,
Echoes of laughter in joy profound.
Hearts intertwined like the branches bare,
In the luminous whispers that float in the air.

As night deepens, the world holds its breath,
In the shimmering stillness, a promise of breadth.
The drifts gleam softly, a canvas pristine,
In the glow of the night, all is serene.

The Calm Before the Gleaming Fall

A hush settles over the forest green,
Nature prepares for the change unseen.
Leaves hang suspended in the soft breeze,
Whispers of autumn rustle through trees.

In the quiet moments before the shift,
Time seems to pause, a delicate gift.
Colors await their chance to ignite,
In the calm before the gleaming light.

The air grows crisp with a hint of spice,
Promises linger of treasures so nice.
Branches adorned with a golden crown,
Awaiting the moment when they'll drift down.

Gentle sighs from the skies above,
Nature's heart beats with the pulse of love.
Sunlight lingers on the edges of day,
In stillness, she gathers, preparing her play.

Underneath skies painted shades of blue,
Lies the calmness that feels ever new.
A moment of grace before colors spill,
In the calm, lies the promise, the thrill.

Fragments of Light on Winter's Sheet

Beneath the veil of a winter's night,
Fragments of light weave a tapestry bright.
Stars twinkle softly in a sea of black,
Guiding the dreams on their silent track.

Crystals form on trees, pure and clear,
Each icy branch holds a story dear.
Whispers of frost paint the world anew,
In delicate patterns of silver and blue.

Footsteps crunch on a canvas of white,
As shadows play in the fading light.
The air breathes magic; each gust a chance,
To twirl with wonder, to shimmer, to dance.

Winter's embrace, a soft, tender hold,
In moments of silence, warmth takes its fold.
Nights stretch longer, yet hearts stay bright,
In fragments of light on winter's sheet.

And as dawn breaks with a soft, golden hue,
The world awakens, refreshed and anew.
Light spills over with a soft, gentle reach,
A promise encased in the lessons it teaches.

Celestial Glow Upon a Blanketing White

Under the canopy of the night so deep,
Celestial wonders lull the world to sleep.
A blanket of white veils the earth below,
With dreams wrapped tightly in soft, silent snow.

Stars twinkle softly, a radiant glow,
Marking the paths of the winds that blow.
The moon graces the sky, a guardian bright,
Casting a spell with her silver light.

The world holds its breath in the stillness found,
Cradled in beauty, a magic profound.
Each snowflake whispers of journeys ahead,
In the celestial glow, all worries are shed.

Winter's embrace, a serene retreat,
In the hush of the night, hearts skip a beat.
Voices of solace in the cool, crisp air,
In a world blanketed with wonder and care.

As dawn approaches, the glow starts to fade,
A canvas adorned with the dreams softly laid.
Yet in the quiet, the promise remains,
In celestial glow, love forever reigns.

Frosted Echoes in the Moonlit Night

In the stillness, whispers glide,
Underneath the stars that bide.
Frozen breath on silver leaves,
Nature's secrets, soft it weaves.

Moonbeams dance on icy streams,
Crystals shimmer, reflecting dreams.
A world draped in velvet white,
Holds the echoes of the night.

Footsteps hush on layered snow,
Where the gentle shadows grow.
Time stands still, wrapped in delight,
In this frosted, joyful sight.

Branches bow beneath the weight,
Silent charms do gently wait.
As the evening breathes its sigh,
Underneath the starry sky.

Voices carried on the breeze,
In this realm where hearts find ease.
Frosted echoes softly sound,
In the night, pure peace is found.

The Gentle Tapestry of Flurries

Whirling softly, white confetti,
Dancing lightly, oh so pretty.
Each flake tells a tale anew,
In this world of muted hue.

A tapestry of dreams unfurl,
As winter winds begin to swirl.
Branches wear a coat of lace,
Harmonies in time and space.

Quiet roads beneath the cloud,
Shrouded softly, winter proud.
Footprints left in fresh-made snow,
Guide the heart where warmth will grow.

Fingers reach to catch the flight,
Of the flurries, soft and light.
Nature paints her fleeting art,
With each flake, she warms the heart.

In the hush, the world is bare,
Yet there's magic in the air.
Each flurry whispers, soft and low,
In this dance of purest glow.

Radiant Stillness of the Falling Tide

In twilight's glow, the waters sing,
Rhythm of waves, a soothing ring.
Glimmers dance where moonlight plays,
In the stillness, hearts find ways.

The tide retreats with gentle grace,
Leaving whispers on the face.
Softly crashing, retreating sighs,
Nature hums beneath the skies.

Calm reflections, nighty hue,
Magic sparkles, ever new.
Salt-kissed breezes weave their lore,
On the shore, our spirits soar.

Seashells scattered, tales untold,
In their whispers, moments hold.
Radiant stillness fills the air,
With every wave, with every prayer.

As the stars begin to fade,
In the silence dreams are made.
Falling tide, a soft goodbye,
In the night, we learn to fly.

Serene Glimpses in a Frosted World

In the hush of morning's light,
Every breath feels pure and bright.
A frosted world, untouched and still,
Nature's canvas, sheer goodwill.

Gentle whispers, crisp and clear,
Echo softly in our ear.
Glimpses of a silent grace,
In the stillness, we embrace.

Shapes of wonder, white and fine,
Crafted beautifully by time.
Trees adorned in shimmering glow,
Glistening softly, peace in tow.

Footprints lead where dreams do dwell,
In this frosted, tranquil spell.
Every moment, pure and bright,
Holds the magic of the night.

In the serene, we find our way,
Through frosted realms, where hearts can play.
Every glance, a treasure, unfurled,
In the beauty of this world.

Twilight's Crystal Lullaby

In twilight's gaze, the stars awake,
Whispers dance on the gentle lake.
A soft embrace, the night unfolds,
Dreams are woven, tales retold.

Silhouettes of trees stand tall,
Moonbeams touch, a silken thrall.
The world draped in silver mist,
In this moment, time is kissed.

Echoes of dusk, a serene vibe,
Colors blend, they softly jibe.
A lullaby of deep repose,
As twilight's beauty gently grows.

Crickets sing a soothing tune,
Underneath the watchful moon.
Nature's heartbeat, slow and deep,
In crystal dreams, the world will sleep.

As shadows fade, new colors bloom,
A quiet grace within the gloom.
Rest now, heart, and breathe in peace,
In twilight's arms, let worries cease.

The Soft Breath of Winter's Caress

A blanket white on fields once green,
Soft breath of winter, calm and serene.
The world holds still in frosty breath,
As nature whispers tales of death.

Snowflakes dance on the chilled air,
Each one unique, a fleeting prayer.
Branches bow beneath their weight,
In silent beauty, they contemplate.

The hearth's glow warms the frigid night,
Families gather, hearts alight.
Sipping cocoa, laughter flows,
In the quiet, love only grows.

Footprints dash on the crisp white ground,
Echoes of joy, a fleeting sound.
Children play in the glistening snow,
Chasing dreams where cold winds blow.

As day gives way to evening's sigh,
Stars awaken in the velvet sky.
The soft breath of winter's embrace,
Cradles all in gentle grace.

Dappled Radiance on Snowy Fields

Morning breaks with a golden glance,
Sunlight sparkles, a joyful dance.
Dappled radiance on snow's pure face,
Nature's palette, a warm embrace.

Whispers of wind through the frosty trees,
Softly rustling like gentle seas.
Each flake glimmers in light's sweet kiss,
A moment captured, a touch of bliss.

Footsteps crunch on the fresh white crust,
In winter's beauty, we place our trust.
Fields stretch wide under sky so blue,
In every shadow, a secret hue.

Fluffy clouds drift in lazy rays,
Winter's magic in soft displays.
The sun dips low, day's warmth retreats,
While twilight dances in rhythmic beats.

The evening brings a gentle chill,
Stars peer out, as night grows still.
The field transforms, a serene sight,
In dappled radiance, soft and bright.

Moonlit Poise in a Frozen World

The moon hangs high, a silver sphere,
Casting shadows that softly adhere.
In frozen stillness, the world stands bold,
A quiet poise that never grows old.

Crystals shimmer on branches bare,
Each frigid breath hangs in the air.
A hush descends, the night is deep,
In moonlit poise, the earth will sleep.

Across the lake, a mirror bright,
Reflecting dreams in the soft night light.
Birds hush their song, tucked in their nests,
Nature's heart finds peace and rest.

White peaks rise like ghosts from the past,
Lending grace to the night held fast.
The world is wrapped in a soft embrace,
In frozen beauty, time has no race.

Amidst the quiet, one can hear,
The whispering winds, always near.
In this frozen world, magic swirls,
As the moonlight dances, life unfurls.

www.ingramcontent.com/pod-product-compliance
Ingram Content Group UK Ltd.
Pitfield, Milton Keynes, MK11 3LW, UK
UKHW051313181224
452382UK00022B/275